Intentionally Here

Here's what happens when you show up for yourself.

SHAKEYLA M. INGRAM

DEDICATION

Intentionally Here is dedicated to my grandmothers,
Gloria Marie Smith-Ingram and Catherine Johnson

CONTENTS

Q: Is showing up for yourself difficult at times?

A: Yes

1

THE ANATOMY OF INTENT

Intent, as a noun, is defined as a usually clearly formulated or planned intention or the state of mind with which an act is done. Then "intent" as an adjective is defined similarly to "having the mind, attention, or will concentrated on something or some end or purpose."

Growing up, my dad would always say to me, "Keyla, think about things before you speak." He would say this because I had a habit of saying the first thing that came to mind without really processing it. After multiple times of my dad stressing the importance of me thinking about things before saying them out loud, I began to be intentional about it. In this practice, I began to catch myself before I said something and would attempt to clearly think it through. What I learned is that if I actually thought something through, I'd come up with an answer of understanding, and then I would be able to have a much more different dialogue with my dad.

When we think about the anatomy of intent and begin to understand how it shapes our next steps in our future, we will begin to understand how important it is to be intentional. For most people, when they wake up in the morning, it's an intentional habit to check their phones and social media. For me, when I'm being intentional about how I want to structure my day, I'm typically intentional about not checking my phone until I'm dressed up and ready to begin my day. The intent of this practice is to maintain my peace of mind when I wake up in the morning. This helps me work toward remaining calm throughout my day, and because part of my morning routine is to meditate, I'm able to let go of things with ease, especially when they're posing a threat to my peace of mind.

In 2017, I remember living in Atlanta, GA, and having a pretty okay job, but I wanted to do something that I loved, which was production design. I'm just always amazed by the art of it. In short, I met Oprah Winfrey on the set of Henrietta Lacks while simultaneously having thoughts of really pursuing this career. Having worked all day and night, I got home around two in the morning, exhausted, took a shower, and spent most of the time in the shower, thinking of how I was going to land this opportunity. I got out of the shower, wrapped myself in my house coat, grabbed my laptop, and began to email production designers (about 20) whose work I was familiar with (e.g., movies that had received a lot of attention). A few months passed, and I still hadn't heard anything, not even from my follow-ups, so I gave up. I felt like maybe it wasn't meant for me.

After a few months later, something

unexpected happened. I ended up in Oprah Winfrey's presence once again; she was giving a speech to a graduating class, so I paid attention. In her speech, she talked about commitment. She stated, "If you make a commitment, a conscious intention to be committed to the work that you do to the relationships that you have, your life will unfold with such beauty and grace through that commitment." As I listened to her, I began to think about what my commitment was, which was to figure out how to get my foot in the door of Production Design. Because I'm a thinker, thanks to my dad, I sometimes overthink things, which then leads me to start thinking myself down a rabbit hole of doubt. Shakeyla, that's impossible; you can't just become a production designer. You didn't even finish college; what do you know about set-design? How do you know you have what it takes? I mean, I exhaust myself with my own thoughts. My subconscious mind helped me stop the madness I was creating and brought my attention back to the speech. After I was done working and was extremely tired again, I went home, took a shower, and once again brought myself back to the thoughts of production design. I thought to myself, "This is my second time meeting this woman, and I feel empowered to really pursue this." So I went back to the drawing board and began to think about my plan a bit differently. I approached it by identifying my favorite movies that I watch nonstop—and still do to this day—which includes Hotel Rwanda, The Color Purple, Mandela: Long Walk To Freedom, and Malcolm X. Surprisingly, two of those movies (Hotel Rwanda, and Mandela: Long Walk To Freedom) had the same production designer, so I sat there on my bed, and I wrote him a very long email about how I was interested in shadowing him and learning about this industry. At this point, I wasn't thinking too much about my job or my marketing business, but a part of me felt like I didn't have to because I knew he wouldn't respond.

Around 11:30 p.m. that evening, I received a response from him asking me a wealth of questions that I did not know the answers to, but I responded with what I did know and expressed what I didn't know. He then immediately replied and said that I was the first person out of hundreds who had reached out to him seeking mentorship to own up to not knowing all of the answers. For him, that was

—

honorable and made him feel comfortable taking me under his wing. Over the course of a few months, he had given me assignments such as things to study, watch, or think about, and then one day, he proposed an opportunity to me. He expressed that he mentioned my name to some producers on a new TV series he was the production designer for, and there was a potential opportunity for me to shadow him. Me being shocked and nervous, I immediately told him, "No, I'm not ready for that," but he insisted. The dates he sent for me to come conflicted with my schedule, so I had to let him know I couldn't go. About a week later, I got extremely pissed off at work, and I knew I had vacation days, so I put in a request for vacation for the dates I knew I could take off, and I emailed him the dates and told him if the opportunity was still available, I would like come. He replied with, "Those dates are perfect. The producers have also signed off on you getting paid to come." And I can't forget to mention that he informed me in this email that the show was part of Shonda Rhimes Studios! At this point, I'm calling one of my girlfriends, April, going crazy because I was excited, scared, and broke! I remember April saying to me, "Girl, watch. As soon as we hang up the phone, someone is going to sponsor your trip." Needless to say, in the middle of our conversation, I texted another friend about it, who only asked me when I would be leaving. And before I knew it, they were telling me to check my email because they had booked my flight. At that moment, I just sat there crying because it had dawned on me that this was my opportunity. I was intentional about it.

I didn't know what I was really getting myself into. I just knew this was something that I wanted to do. I saw myself doing it, and I believed I could do it. This is within the anatomy of intent—deciding how you see yourself showing up and choosing what intentional action that will benefit you on your path. Each day we wake up, we have to choose if we will be kind or if we'll be working on a behavior that we've wanted to change.

Being intentional is the foundation for being the version of yourself that you desire to be.

Practice:

Take some time to reflect and think
about your future.

Think about what intentional actions you are
willing to make to reach the version of yourself
that you envision.

NOTES

2

INTENTIONALLY HER

I recall watching a comedy family movie where a white man expressed his condolences to a black man, saying, "My condolence for your loss. The black woman is a staple to the American black family—heck, to all American families. I don't know a person who wasn't raised by black women; even I was raised by one…." I chuckled at the comedic expression of the statement, but I acknowledged the truth behind the joke. Women, particularly black women, are staples of the American society.

In today's societal make-up, and as history has shared in the past, women have had to forge a place of right—a right that is so easily given to men simply because of their gender—with the hope of having value beyond being the sole nurturer of their families. Today, we live in a society where we're asked to provide our "pronouns" for the sake of equality and freedom to be addressed as you wish. For me, I choose to be proudly recognized for what I was born as—a woman, female, she, HER.

Born to Ricky and Sherrill, I had a strong influence on my upbringing from my grandparents, Arthur and Gloria Ingram and Catherine Johnson. My dad is extremely handy and a problem solver. My mom is intellectual and outgoing. They both have a heart of gold for others. My grandfather is your silent supporter—he'd linger in the background, making things happen and supporting people in many ways. And if you knew him, then you knew he loved his girls. Lastly, grandmothers… Whew, chile, those ladies had a great impact on my life! My grandma Gloria was a barber and co-owned the Ramsey Street Barbershop with my grandad, Arthur. Most days, my grandmother ran the shop by herself. She had a strong sense of humor and could talk to you for hours. I appreciated her endurance, her unshakable stature, and, mostly, her love for people. Catherine, my grandmamma, was all about hospitality; she took care of people no matter what, which came from a place growing up because she had to — she was a provider. The very thing I love about these people is that they love their families and are not perfect and do not try to be. In addition, I'd like to believe the presence of these giants in my life helped me become the intentional woman I am today.

So, let's talk a bit more about two of my ladies, my grandma, and my grandmama. As I said earlier on, my grandma was a barber, and a fine one at that. She was highly respected as a leading lady in the male-dominated industry she worked and owned a business. Growing up and spending most of my time at the barbershop with her, through my observations, she taught me how to handle people. My grandma was very intentional about how she communicated with her customers; simply put, a lot of men often felt like they could say whatever they wanted to say to her, and she'd just take it. That wasn't the case with her; she would give you a good cursin' and would send you on your way with love. I must say, I'm still working on this because I'd feel more comfortable sending you on your way. During the time my grandma ran her barbershop, it wasn't every day you'd see this feisty, short, afro-wearing, ring on every finger, cigarette-smoking woman standing up to any man that crossed the threshold of disrespect. And because she knew who she was to her core, those who messed around with her and found out grew to have much respect for her and would do anything for her. My grandma was big on creating opportunities for the underdog, and most times, we'd be looking at her like she was crazy. Growing up, the local homeless people, like Stickman and Wolfman, would be at the house on the weekend fixing things around the house for a couple of bucks. My grandma would pray to God they didn't steal anything because my grandad would already be hotter than fish grease, knowing that she'd had them at the house. She didn't care if she saw felons or homeless people that needed help, so that's what she did. Now, I know you're probably reading this thinking, "How dare Shakeyla think that about homeless people?" So let me remind you, this is from the perspective of a kid growing up. And in all actuality, my experiences with my grandmother at her barbershop helped me understand that not all homeless people are bad. Some just want help, whether it be with mental health or an opportunity to be productive, or they just want to be seen as human.

Looking back, I think one of my most prized experiences with my grandma was going to the rest home with her while she cut the residents' hair. I was the honorary snack helper, and I made sure "we" ate lots of jello. Another would be her mentoring women coming up in the industry because she didn't just mention them; she was like a mother to them. If they needed a place to stay, she moved them into the house and was intentional about getting them to a place of sustainability. Now, she wasn't perfect; she had her struggles. My grandma struggled with her own mental health. Growing up, I never understood how she took care of us, cooked dinner almost every night, and still got up every single day, went to work, and endured. Honestly, it wasn't until I became intentional that I understood her experiences.

—

My grandmamma, Catharine, was a homemaker; she raised her three boys on her own while also running her own hospice care. Her home was her business, where she had in-home patients, two of whom I'd never forget: Mr. James and Mr. Sinclair. I grew up watching her be there for her boys and take care of her patients. While both of my grandmothers were no-nonsense, my grandmother had a different way of communicating. While she could give a good cursing', she could also implement a ton of understanding, love, and was a strong voice of reason. My grandmama ensured there was never a need that went unmet, and this just wasn't in my case. Her door was always open, figuratively, and literally. I've never needed to have a key to her house. During the weekdays, if a kid was over and she was making dinner, she'd be sure to ask, "You staying for dinner?" Or during holidays like Christmas, you can bet all the kids in the neighborhood had a gift neatly wrapped and waiting for them. I can recall one time I counted 200 wrapped gifts and was puzzled, trying to figure out where she had the time to wrap them all. This was my grandmamma, an intentional, hospitable, and nurturing woman. It didn't stop there; my

—

grandmother birthed two boys of her own and adopted a third and raised him as hers. My uncle's biological parents had recently moved to the states from Korea and were living in New Jersey. Not long after moving to the states, his biological dad left, leaving his mom to raise my uncle on her own. My grandma's twin sister introduced my uncle's biological mom to my grandmamma, and they became friends. Realizing her struggle to raise him, my grandmama offered to take him in, and she did just that. She raised him as her own, and I will tell you, she was intentional about his upbringing as a black woman living in a predominantly white community called Haymount. Raising two of her own black boys and a Korean child did not make things easier for her; however, I watched her be intentional about the impact she made within the community while raising us. She never walked in fear. I always saw her walk in a stance of belonging!

These are just a few examples of how my grandmothers' intentionality helped influence me to be intentional. Today, the intentional woman has much work ahead of her if she's to succeed, just like in my grandmothers' case. But I believe the difference is that my grandmothers didn't have the pressure of social media highlighting certain aspects of women to make them appear mindless, bitchy, or emotional. Oh, and specifically for black women, we get the red carpet rolled out with anger, difficulty, or aggression.

There are so many stereotypes about women, particularly black women, that they have become too far and few to see when we are celebrated. Why can't we be recognized as a winning woman, a happy woman, a balanced, helpful, and intentional—the things that we actually are and not just what people want us to appear to be for their own social benefit? We can, in a very easy way, be intentional about the things we do. Be the intentional woman who says, "You know what? I can't be all the great things I dream of being if I don't uplift my fellow intentional sister." And this can also apply to men. I like to call these "Goal Friends," where Intentional Women and Intentional Men are not only intentional about affirming themselves but are just as intentional about affirming others.

—

Who is an Intentional Woman? She is a woman who has decided to be intentional about where she takes her life, her goals, her dreams, and her skills, in addition to being intentional about how she gets there.

Practice:

Let's say you've decided that you want to be an Intentional Woman. Use your intentional actions to share what life looks like for you.

NOTES

3

INTENTIONALLY YOUNG, GIFTED & BLACK

As a kid, I always felt I was misunderstood, and I needed to find ways to fit in even more, which made things even worse—well, at least at the time, it felt like hell. I started to feel this way in middle school, especially when I decided I wanted to stop running track and play football. Something about running at the time in my life made no sense, but what did make sense was being a girl wanting to play football and make tackles. I was judged beyond belief.

—

When it came down to tryouts, I pushed and worked hard. I had to outwork the boys and prove myself to the coaches, who already didn't want me there. I'll never forget the day I made the team; boys cried not because they didn't make it but because they couldn't understand how I made it over them and didn't know how in the hell they were going to tell their dads the news. For a moment, I felt bad seeing those dads and grandads march up to the field with their kids yelling at the coaches, mostly because their pride had been shattered, turning them into sexists and entitled parents—because I worked hard to earn my spot on the team and their boy shouldn't have to prove anything over a girl. Without even realizing it, this was the beginning of "her."

While my mom was fully on board with letting me play, my dad and my grandad made it clear they didn't fully agree with it but would support me, which they did. All hell would break loose when I started, with teammates confused as to why I was starting over them, and I'd be thinking, "Um, because I'm the best defensive tackle you have, and I make pretty damn good hits. That's why!" But the coaches were ten toes down when it came to me, mostly because they decided not to focus on my sex and instead see me as a player. Moving forward into the season, being in school was not the best. Although I made the "homies list" with the guys in school, I made the "rejects list" with the girls, and it was not fun. They talked about me in front of me and even pulled me into the friend groups just to embarrass me at the opportune time, but I didn't let that deter me.

My grandmothers were women who didn't let other people's opinions stop them from doing something, and I had no intention of leaving the team because some students wanted to bully me. In addition to me being a football player, people assumed I was supposed to "dress the part" or be a lesbian. Nope. I was cute, girly, and liked boys, which made them (especially the girls) dislike me even more! Here's the thing, I was very intentional about making sure I made the team because I knew this would not only be a challenge for me, but it would be a challenge to break societal norms — which is my most favorite activity. I also knew that I didn't want to hold myself back from anything I wanted to do. I guess you can

—

say this was the start to my decision about wanting to be an Intentional Woman.

As I mentioned earlier, I simply wasn't raised to be any other way. You'll see that statement a lot in this book. Lol.

Much like the experience my grandmother had gaining respect from her customers, I gained respect from my teammates, and to be honest, I didn't care if they did or not. Because of my grandparents and parents, I had a good sense of who I was and where I was coming from. I knew I was young and gifted, and everyone could see I was a black female. Nina Simone's song "Young, Gifted, and Black" is a go-to for me because these three words paired together have more adversity than I'd care to acknowledge, and even in the face of adversity, you're expected to be resilient.

To be young, gifted, black, broken-down word by word means this to me.

To be young is not a measure of age but a measure of perspective. Despite the fact that I'm still young, life experience may bring a horizon of wisdom, even though wisdom is mostly associated with age. But doesn't have to be entirely true. Hence the saying, "You're wise beyond your years." A measure of being young in perspective is the ability to not see your age as a hindrance to what you can do or how far you can go. There's this notion that the older we get, the slower we get or adapt the mindset of "I'm too old to try and reach this dream." There are numerous negative nuances that take away the youthful wide-eyed dare to dream and imaginative mindset that you typically experience when you're young.

Being gifted gives you the space to act on this "bump my age," I can still make it happen by drawing from that young-at-heart perspective. When I decided I wanted to play football, I knew what my gifts were and how they would help me be intentional about achieving my goal. I took those gifts and my intentional actions and showed up every day ready to be this intentional, young, gifted, black girl in a male-dominated sport, breaking social norms. Your gifts and mindset are what will carry you through this intentional journey you've set out for. The very moment you shift into long-term self-doubt or of a negative party, you'll quickly see the side effects of this shift, and it won't feel good. As human beings, we must honor and give space to frustration, setbacks, and just things that don't feel good on this journey. A skill that I would like to gift you if you haven't begun to practice it already is Emotional Intelligence. This is the ability to manage and understand our emotions and recognize the influence of others' emotions around us, in addition to the influence our emotions can have on ourselves while striving to be intentional. First, I must admit, it is an everyday practice that you don't always get right because we're human. However, I can share that this came in handy for me when I mentioned I felt bad for the guys who didn't make the football team and when I was being bullied for being different.

For those of the culture, to be black creates its own realm of meaning. For the scope of this conversation, even though I want to dismiss the negative experiences associated with being black, I simply cannot. While society celebrates black people's culture through appropriation, we that are of the culture must utilize our youthfulness of heart and gifts in the hope of overcompensating that we are black, especially in the workplace! While our gifts make space for us, being black creates hurdles like no other. And because of this, I choose to be solely proud of being black. Not because I believe I cannot change it, nor because it's the culturally fit thing to do, but because being proud to be young, gifted, and BLACK creates space for that pride to be multiplied for generations to come.

Even though I recognize the hurdles people of the culture have to experience because they're black, I've always been adaptable enough to carve my own path to supporting my livelihood, much like my grandparents. This would always leave me facing the question: "Who does she think she is?" And a lot of times when I'd hear that question, I'd begin to hear in my mind Nina Simone singing, "Oh, but my joy of today is that we can all be proud to say, 'to be young, gifted and black is where it's at.' Personally, I don't like societal norms, and any effort to get me to conform or accept a norm as to how black people are treated is just not a part of my intentional lifestyle. Most times, I chuckle because I'd most certainly have an answer for them—though it probably would've gotten me associated with the typical stereotypes had I expressed to them who I believed myself to be, not what I thought myself to be. I've also learned very quickly that, though I am this beautifully brilliant young, gifted, and black being, I also don't owe a damn soul any explanation of my existence because that's between them and God if they have grave concerns about my existence. In addition, sometimes, when people ask rhetorical questions, it's okay to give a silent answer, like, "Yeah, you ask who I thought I was. Well, I can show you better than I can tell you."

Now though I grew up in a family full of proud black people, internally, I struggled to find my place within the "black culture." Seeing so many mixed views and different ways the black community would be treated left me trying hard to maintain my blackness and not come off as acting like a white girl, as some would say, just so I could get fair treatment. I mean, I had white best friends up until high school, when I started attending a majority-black school. I also was perceived to be a bit weird; apparently, my interests as a black person didn't align with the stereotypical black person agenda, which ignited the infamous ass backward comment, "You're cute for a dark-skinned girl," leaving me to shrink and reply with a thank you, affirming it was okay for that to be said to me when it wasn't and when my true thoughts were, "No, fool. I'm cute, period." BUT as a young, gifted, and black person, standing up for yourself and challenging someone to correct them is very "divisive," which would very quickly make you the aggressive black person.

Although, on the surface, it appeared I acted like a "white girl" to some, which is disrespectful as hell. My life experiences aligned with what we call "black culture," but forget all that. I'm young, and I'm gifted as hell, and to put the icing on the cake, I'm black as hell, which I'm very proud of. Whether society wants to admit it or not, they see that as a triple threat. Why is it that society can't accept that black people don't all carry a tone of voice that doesn't come off as threatening, aggressive, or educated?

42

From my perspective, being young, gifted, and black does come with some harsh realities and valuable lessons, both of comfort and discomfort, but to be honest, it's where it's at.

Practice:

As you develop this intentional you,
what are three things that bring you comfort
and discomfort but are also things you are
proud to be?

And share why those three.

NOTES

4

THE INTENT OF BROKENESS

Earlier, I mentioned some things about emotional intelligence, discomfort in being who you are, and just the everyday lifecycle of having to be intentional and "keeping your stuff together," Honestly, it's impossible to be on this journey of being intentional about where you're taking your life and think you'll be able to keep it all intact. When I experienced my second depression, which was more severe than my first, I fully grasped how I was able to be intentional about the broken state I was in.

I was a young, gifted, black female professional living in Atlanta, GA, when I began to feel unsettled about where I was in life and chile… my relationship. My job was applying so much pressure that I would look up and see that I was being taken advantage of because I was young and gifted, and I would wonder why in the hell I was this amazing woman but couldn't seem to be of value to a man who was single— yeah, I said it. I never bit that apple, but it did play harsh roll in my self-confidence. Then, on top of all of this, my grandmama's health was declining, and I couldn't be home as much as I wanted to. When I am experiencing a hardship, I tend to freeze—more like shut completely down. Depending on how serious it is, there are a lot of things I do when this happens. If it's something small, but I still feel inconvenienced about it, I'll call my best friend, and he'll tell me, "Alright, you've got 30 minutes to be down about it." And I'll use my 30 minutes to cry, yell, talk cash shit, or just go take a nap. But for what I was experiencing, everything was building up, and I was going down—and I went down hard. I remember what put the icing on the cake was that it was

—

Mother's Day weekend, and I needed to go home and see my grandmama. I attempted to express this to my supervisor at the time, and their response was, "If you want to keep your job, then you'll tell your family you'll get there after the weekend." Hearing that, it was like something in me had broken. I was already feeling alone, and my last living grandmother was not doing well. I began to decline; I stopped eating, and after a while, I stopped bathing, I stopped going into the office to work, and I wasn't getting back to my clients for my business. At best, the most I could do was lie in bed and cry or go get on the couch and cry. One day, I went into the office and decided that I couldn't do it anymore. I didn't know what specifically it was that I couldn't do; I just knew something had to give. My state declined to the point where my best friends had to come down from Michigan and North Carolina to see about me, and my parents were telling me to just come home. Even a close friend that lives up the street across from me would come over and let me cry on her lap and just be there for me when I felt I didn't need to be by myself.

—

I remember the day I called up the director in our DEI department and went into her office to sit on the floor behind her desk and ball my everything out. I didn't know her well enough to be doing this; I just knew I needed help, and I was too broken to fully help myself. We talked, and she asked me if I had ever talked to a therapist, and I said no. She referred me to a black male therapist, and I remember how uncomfortable I felt talking with him. It was through my journaling that I realized because of my experience with black men at that point; I just didn't trust them as a whole. So, I had to make a decision that if I wanted to get better and get the help I needed, I had to be vulnerable with this man, whose job was to help me find my way out of this brokenness. So the next day, I went in, and I swear I just laid on the floor crying, and he sat on the floor on the other side, waiting for me to finish. It was at that moment that I was able to figure out what I was feeling in my state—it was resentment. My therapist could've sat in his chair and watched me cry, but he came down to where I was. I was resentful toward my supervisor, who didn't at least feel my pain and concern for my grandmother's health. I was resentful toward the men who wanted to lie to me about being single. And I resented myself for making decisions that I thought would've put me ahead of certain yet significant goals. After about four sessions of just crying, we finally began to dig in. Very early on, he noticed that I needed to get out of the job I had because it was not only becoming detrimental my mental health but also to my physical health. He placed me on a 30-day medical leave, and with that, I decided to spend those 30 days at home in Fayetteville, NC. I remember everyone at work asking me what I was going to do on this break, and I told them I was going to go get in bed with my grandmama. I got home on July 1, and I began to make progress with coming out of the depressive state I was in. I was spending time with my mom, dad, and best friends and was able to be vulnerable with my grandmama and share what I was going through. Soon, my overall health began to improve…

On July 21, 2018, my world stopped, the progress I was making was reset, and I went back to square one of my depression. That was the day my grandmama passed away. Just when I thought there was hope to make it past where

I was, it quickly went away. Here I was, having just gotten home twenty days ago, trying to get myself healthy, and now I was faced with planning a funeral. This is where you start to think God has joked because this cannot be life. Yet, it is! In the midst of planning my grandmother's funeral, I felt like I was broken into very small pieces and had no way of putting myself back together. Not to mention I was still battling this very severe depression. I recall calling up one of my best friends and telling her I just needed to come over. I went to her house, literally walked myself into the ground, and lay down on her living room floor with my face on her carpet, crying my eyes out. At that moment, she knew what I needed. She knew I just needed to be. She didn't bother me. She kept doing whatever she was doing around the house. She brought me some Kleenex, of course, and set it down beside me. But she let me get it out. In this process of being broken down to where I felt like I was in the negatives, I learned the importance of reaching out when you need people to be there for you when you cannot be there for yourself.

You're probably reading this and thinking,

"This is too damn much!" and at the time, it was. But coming out of it, I learned the intent of being broken. When we are going through tough stuff, we tend to fight against it in a way that makes it ten times harder to come out of it. To be resilient, strong, talented, courageous, and all of the glorious things we see ourselves showing up as when we're going through things or even just fine. We must allow ourselves to break! When I decided to allow myself to break, I put an intention behind it. My intention was to meet the woman on the other side of what I was going through. I knew there was so much more to me to let this be my final moment in life. I needed to break, and I needed to allow my goal friends and family to help put me back together. See, having a goal friend is more than having someone to help you meet your business goal or your weight loss goal. Goal friends can show up however you want them to. Now, there are times when you may experience a different kind of broken state, like being broken from a love connection, falling out with a family member or close friend, or being undervalued in your work environment, and the list goes on. And there's a way to win every time: you must break with an intention because I'll be damned if myself, you, or any

—

other person just allow life to whoop us up in any kind of way without us getting our lick back.

When you've allowed yourself to break with intent, it's only a matter of time before you bounce back. For me, it took about five months; I will never forget it. I was sitting at a holiday party when I took a cute selfie and stared at it, and then ran to the bathroom to cry—because I had met her! I had met the woman I set the intention to meet on the other side of what I had been through. I remember telling a close friend when I was still in Atlanta, GA, that I saw a woman in a white dress, and that's who I needed to meet. Well, y'all, I was wearing a bomb white dress, and it was super cute. I didn't even know what to do with myself. Lol. After all of that, I decided to move back home, and I did something unimaginable… chile… ran for local office and won. So here I was now, a whole city councilwoman representing a city of 200,000 citizens, and the youngest member on my board at the time. Let me tell you, I thought it would be very easy until I realized I stepped in to the lion's den of politics and that and that not all folk who look like you share the same interest as you. I felt like some of the people I was serving with were literally trying to break me, and to be honest, I was breaking fast, but we shall talk about that later. Just know I found myself again having allow myself to break with an intent to unshakably serve my people. And I did just that…

Practice:

Think about a time you've been broken or are currently experiencing a broken state, and you didn't feel like you could see your way out of it.

What is an intention you would have or want to attach to coming out of this broken state?

Now think of your goal friends or family members who you can allow yourself to break with.

Who are they?

How do you want them to show up for you?

NOTES

5

LOVING INTENTIONALLY

Dr. Martin Luther King Jr stated, "I have decided to stick with love. Hate is too great a burden to bear." And while it's true. I've seen people use this for their own benefit, especially after they've been active members in hurting someone. For a brief second, let's talk about f*ck boys. I had a fair show of them. In one of my first and serious relationships, I experienced what I thought would be my "happily ever after," and was I wrong? The man did everything under the sun and moon except be faithful. It was just horrible, and what made it so bad was that I was gullible beyond belief. The relationship ended with me on his porch with blood coming from my face because I used my words to cut him after finding out he was in the streets playing daddy to a kid that wasn't even his and was basically in two relationships, so he used his hands to cut me. I got over that relationship, I told myself that the rest of my 20s were for me and only me. I did that as an excuse to be like, "Yeah, I'm young and living my life like it's golden." When the truth was, I was scared to even let anyone close to my heart, and I didn't benefit from it at all.

There are times when we experience something traumatic, and we freeze. We analyze it and figure out how to not let it happen again. For me, acting like I wanted to live my best single life seemed like the right move, but I had much rather been interested in being a housewife raising kids. Instead, I became single and invested in my work life, with little to no time for men. I also feel I should attach the fact that I grew up watching my mom and dad argue and my grandparents. So, while it looked to be normal, I didn't want it to be my normal. After about two years of living my best life, I decided to give this guy a chance. He was cool, respectful, and responsible, and a family guy… oh, and he had a son, but I looked past that with the quickness, and we hung out for a while. I remember one day, I was at his house, and we watched football late into the night. He claimed he didn't feel comfortable with me driving home and offered that I sleep in his bed. Well, something interesting happened at that moment, and my brain immediately calculated how many reasons I should not stay there because, to me, it felt like we were getting too close. It was like my heart sent an SOS alert to my brain and was like, "Hell naw, girl, we gotta get outta here," and so I did. I got right back into being overly vested in my work life, and we eventually fell off. When I realized I had dropped the ball with him, I had to have a talk with myself because you don't just come across men like him.

The talk I had went a little something like this: "Okay, Shakeyla, you know you want to receive genuine love, and you know you want someone who wants to be loved. Why are you sabotaging yourself like that?" And as I mentioned earlier, I was scared!! And honestly, I couldn't answer myself. I was watching a show or movie one day, and this couple loved each other unconditionally. One of them passed away, and I could feel the other person's pain, and in watching this, I realized that with love, pain is inevitable; it's only a matter of what kind of pain you experience within it. So, I found myself making another choice, and that choice was to love, but with some intention behind it, and here's why. When it came down to my love life, I decided that no matter what relationship didn't work out, I wanted to keep my heart open to love. And in my family, we know some family members that be doing the most; hell, you and I may just be one of them, but with family, I decided that before I let any other family member cause me pain, I would love them from a distance. Also, in my career, I've had people who decided they were just not going to like me or wanted to find reasons to make me look bad. Baby, I got nothing but love for you because if I didn't choose to love these people, I'd be in jail for assault because, once again, you would not play with my kindness of my heart and think I won't get my lick back. I can recall having colleagues that I

—

did not like to go through things personally with, so I would call them to check on them, and they would be shocked that I did that. Mostly because they know how shitty they were to me, but this is what I truly believe, and it is that "God don't play about his kids." The only thing I must do is love, and God will handle everything else. I also can recall feeling bad for these miserable people who decided to spend a good chunk of their time not liking me and coming up with things to make me look bad or ways to hurt me. I felt bad because, obviously, they don't have goal friends, and, more importantly, they cannot possibly have people in their lives who love them, and if they do, they don't know half the ignorant stuff they're doing.

I can honestly say being intentional about loving and opening my heart to love may not have gotten me a man because a sistah is still single, but it has given me a community and family that love me and allow me to love them back!

Practice:

Have you ever closed your heart off because
of the pain that comes from loving?

Let's think about why you closed your heart
and the benefits you thought you would gain
from it.

Did it help or hurt you even more?

If it helped you, explain.
If it hurt you, explain.

Then think about the ways you could have
benefited from being intentional about loving

NOTES

6

THE INTENT OF A LEADER

To be a leader means to be a person who leads or commands a group, organization, or country. To lead means to act as an example for others to follow, and to have intent is to have a purpose for something. So, by these concepts, there are millions of leaders in the world right now, and all of them have an intention behind their leadership. Let's look at some examples. We have a former president who led their followers to believe an election was rigged and stolen and wanted everyone to believe everything negative said about them was fake news. Then you have the late and great John Lewis, who led and urged people to get into good trouble in the fight against injustice. And on a smaller scale, you have a third-grade student who is leading a school effort for all kids to have a friend who is 78 years old, encouraging their peers that it's never too late to achieve their goals.

Now that we've laid out the various types of leadership, let's jump back to when I was in middle school and was trying out for the football team. Even at that moment, I was indirectly showing other girls that we can do and be more than what our gender says we are to do. Even when I got to high school, I remember heading up the Teen Democrats, and coincidentally, it was President Obama's first election to the presidency, and I would not be old enough to vote by the time the election rolled around. So, I asked myself, "How can I make an impact in this historic election?" I was not concerned with being a leader; I just knew I wanted to make me not having a vote count. I had a car and driver's permit, and I had friends. So, after school, we'd get in my car and would go to the Democratic Headquarters, do our homework, then phone bank and canvass. I would even drag them with me to the locally held candidate events that were happening too, and when election day came, I remember hounding everyone and making sure they took their butts to go vote! While I didn't have a set intention of leading, it ended up happening because I wanted my vote to count even though I couldn't vote. Moving forward, my efforts caught a lot of attention, and I was gifted tickets to President Obama's Inauguration and the Neighborhood Ball…

Fast forward to the present day. As a councilwoman serving in my hometown of Fayetteville, NC, when I got sworn to office, my intention for serving was to show up as me, and while people did not like that, what I wanted was little for girls growing up in the city to know that you don't always have to mold yourself into something you're not for the sake of a position or to simply fit in. In my opinion, the shit was played out, but I took some hits showing up as myself. I had to realize that

—

when you're a strong, young woman living life by your own rules, you intimidate a lot of people, but that shouldn't be a problem, and I would suggest to you that you not let it become your problem. Because when you do, you start doing this thing called "shrinking," and that is truly for the birds. If you don't know what shrinking is, it's when you take the bomb-ass person that you are and find the smallest jar possible, and stuff yourself in it to make those that are intimidated by you feel comfortable, giving up everything that wishes you were and doing just for the sake of their egos. And to be honest, this is a black woman's MO ("modus operandi," Latin for "way of operating"). We often find ourselves doing this because we need the job to pay the bills, we don't want someone thinking we're after their job, and in a relationship, a partner may not like it when they're being outshone. This shrinking mechanism keeps us from appearing as a threat to societal standards because your average person is okay with the status quo, but when that status quo starts to shift because of one person, all hell breaks loose, just like when Colin Kaepernick decided not to stand up to show pride in a flag for a country that oppresses black people and people of color.

Americans lost it. This was because the norm was that when the national anthem played and the flags were present, everyone was to stop what they were doing and show "respect and pride" to the American flag, and what you saw after that was a moment where Colin didn't kneel by himself, and there were even people raising their fists. Now, this did cause some issues because they ended up releasing Colin from the franchise; however, he started a movement that is still relevant today.

In 2020, when the COVID-19 pandemic hit us, I was about three months into my term on council and hated every second of it. I could no longer do the things I had planned, and to add to it, friends, family, and constituents were dying. People couldn't go to work to earn an income to pay the rent or bills, families were in need of food, and supplies were scarce. It was truly a scary time. The most interesting thing about this pandemic is that majority of the world has never lived through one. In these trying moments, I had to reevaluate how I needed to show up as a leader who would also speak to me, and I say that because you never want to commit to showing up as something that does not speak to the person that you are—that is how you burn out fast! So, I said, "Okay, my people need reassurance, they need love, and they need to see and feel that they are still cared for." Those things are right up my alley because I am a lover to my core. So I masked up with other PPE and got with churches to deliver food boxes. I also wrote letters of love and acknowledgment, and I hosted virtual parties. I wanted my people to know they were not alone in this. Sometime in the midst of this, something very tragic happened that brought this entire world to its knees! And that was the killing of George Floyd. We all saw how a police officer placed their knee to his neck as the life slipped from his body. The world, just like Colin Kaepernick, Martin Luther King Jr., John Lewis, and many other great leaders of the movement decided enough was enough with the mistreatment and killing of black people. The world stood up and said no more, and still to this date, contribute to what we saw in the demonstrations, protests, looting, and vandalism of property came from a place of anger, rage, and pain. It's not natural to see people be murdered; it's just now

In my hometown, I decided to be with my people; I marched with them, and I cried with them, and we took a hit just like in other cities. Our main hit was the slave market house being sought to burn, which is in the heart of my district. In addition to the fire, protestors began to break windows of businesses, and all I could remember watching in one of the buildings next to it was people trying to get down to a street level so I could stop it. Luckily, I had friends around that stopped me from doing that because they knew I'd get hurt trying to tell a hurt and angry protestor to stop. My heart repeatedly broke every time I heard a glass to a window break and furniture thrown around. After it was all said and done, in tears, I went to the street and tried to clean up what I could that night. The next morning, business owners and community members came together to help restore the businesses, and of course, I followed their lead! It was a very beautiful moment until some business owners began to approach me in anger, accusing me of being the cause of it. Here I was feeling bad for people who looked like me because we continued to endure injustice in every way imaginable and feeling bad for these business owners because they did not deserve to have their businesses torn to pieces, and yet white men had all of the nerves to tower over me with their finger in my face telling me I'm not fit to lead this city and get this: a constituent was so bold enough to pick up their phone and call me a "nigger" because she was not happy with what happened and did not even block her caller ID. I figure that was a proud moment for her, and she obviously felt empowered to do so. Honestly, I felt like giving up. As soon as I hung up the phone, I grabbed one of my friends and went into an alley and cried. This was a time when I did not want to be a leader; what I wanted to say was that y'all can have all of this and be out in the streets protesting.

Being a woman in leadership has its highs and nasty lows. As a woman in leadership, you are expected to dress like a nun and speak like a saint, and you are expected to let the men be right even when they are wrong. Well, I do none of these things, and quite frankly, I do the opposite. See, I told you earlier about the kind of women I grew up with, and you probably recognized they left a remarkable impression on me. Women leaders bring something unique to the table; we tend to be more transformative than men because it stems from the essence of what society deems a woman to do. It was the woman who balanced the checkbook when their husband came home with the checkbook. It was the woman who had to be a doctor when all her children were sick. It was the woman who had to give strategic advice to her husband about how to manage his business. Women have historically been relied on by everyone to have their needs and wants met. It is also the woman who can outperform a man and be more qualified and still be underpaid. As a female leader, I've learned the pros and cons of sticking together with my fellow women leaders. Firstly, we look damn good doing it. Secondly, we are all we've got at times, and when our backs are against the wall, there's nothing like your sister stepping in for you. For instance, I had a situation with a male colleague who was upset with me because I called him out about a decision he made, and then he decided to go on a lying campaign about the direction he took. Well, in his anger and shattered ego, instead of keeping it about business, he decided to try and get personal and said, "I don't talk about how you're out here being booty calls with so and so," and at that moment I wanted to hit them because how

—

dare you try to lie on me to my face. Who does that? So, let's pause right here and break this down. Why do you think he felt it was okay to challenge me that way? Let me help you. First, because I'm young. Second, because I'm single, and third, because I'm a black woman, and for a very long time, people couldn't track what I had going on in my personal life, and what makes it even worse is they denied having said it, but their close friends confirmed it because they went back and talked about it as if they had just gotten one on me. When you're a woman in leadership and men know you're single, they will attempt to see how far they can get with disrespecting you, and what I've learned is you don't need a significant other to lay down the law for how people treat you. You treat people how they treat you.

Practice:

Think about how you've shown up in
leadership or how you want to show up.

What does that look like, and how did you—or
will you—teach people how to treat you?

NOTES

7

INTENTIONALLY HEALING

Healing, just like brokenness, is an uncomfortable space. We know we must heal to get better, but sometimes we are apprehensive about being intentional with our healing because we know there's potential for that wound to be opened back up, which restarts the healing process.

In every chapter of our lives has an intention attached, in those chapters there has to be some healing associated with it. When I decided to open my heart to love, I had to intentionally heal from what made me not want to open my heart. When I wanted to give up on my leadership role, I had to think about what was making me want to quit, and it was mostly because of how I was being treated. If we are not intentional about how we heal, we will not get far. A large part of healing begins with forgiveness, which helps the process more than you know. And let me be clear, I'm talking about genuine forgiveness. If you have to forgive someone or yourself, you must do so with an open heart. We never know how long a healing process can take, as it varies from one person to the other and from one situation to the next, but what we do know is that if we are intentional about it, it will happen. This is a major piece to help you show up for yourself.

When we heal, we begin to gain a new perspective on the situation, person, or entity that may have caused us pain or hurt. You may begin to say, "Hmm, you know what. That's more of a 'them problem' than my problem." Which helps you to forgive and let go. If you're an adult like me, you know that we are always finding new ways to heal. But what remains true is the need to have the intention to heal. Being intentional about your healing process creates space for you to grow intentionally, gain a different outcome, and share your process with others. We don't always want to believe we can heal from something, and honestly, we don't realize we've healed from a situation until it presents itself again. And the way you handle it will trigger something in you to recognize this different response. Through the process of healing, learn to give yourself grace and space to experience it all over again. Whatever it is you're fighting to overcome, let it come up, let it settle in you with the intention to understand it and the understanding to release it because once you've addressed the feeling and explored it, you can then release it. Exploring and releasing helps you be able to express it without feeling all the anger attached to it. Remember, you allowed yourself to break if it was needed in the process. So, for example, after my colleague accused me of being someone's booty call and having experienced another male colleague standing up to me yelling and shouting because I stated what was true, and secretly having meetings to get citizens to file complaints against me… It was real ghetto, but I got to the point where I was so angry for very many reasons, and I held on to it for damn near a year. That year, I began to show up in survival mood, meaning I was on everyone's ass! Which was causing me more pain because it wasn't who I was. I remember being in the office with a colleague who was supporting me as I was preparing to retaliate – I stopped and looked are and said, this isn't how I do things, and she supported my choice. When I realized holding on to that hurt was causing me more harm, I began to start my healing process. I explored what I was feeling and why I was feeling it, and after I did that, I let go. I then expressed how it made me feel to my close friends, and then I attempted to do so with the people who caused the harm. And at that moment, when I was trying to tell them what their actions did while hearing some of their responses it reminded me of that – things like this are unnecessary unless you just need a repeat reminder of needing to trust someone to show you who they are. In short, trust people that continuously show you who they are. Once I finished trying to give them a grace and space to talk through my experience with them and theirs with me, I went back to the goal friends to express how I felt falling the conversation, and honestly, I felt played… because listen, as tough as we want to appear, we don't always need to go through things alone. So now I know who you are; I've chosen to love you from a distance, and I know how to forgive that person even if space or reason were not given to forgive. But to be honest, there's always a reason to forgive and heal. You've been blessed with a life that you are in control of, and I would never want to see time slip away from you because you've allowed a situation or a person to dictate how you show up for yourself.

Practice:

Think about what healing looks like for you
now.

Now think about what you want it to look like
when you are intentionally about healing.

For example, I had to set journey agreements
with myself. One of my agreements were that I
would honor whatever feeling came up and not
push my friends away in when I was dealing
with those feelings. I did this because I used to
feel like I was being a burden if I went to my
friends about it all the time knowing they were
navigating life just like me.

Now, do you allow your goal friends or family
to be there for you in this healing process?
If not, why?

NOTES

8

INTENTIONALLY HERE
A LETTER TO YOU

My dear friend,

I never would have imagined myself writing a book, much like I never would've imaging myself doing and being anything, I set an intention on. While writing this book I recalled times where I reaped the benefits of showing up for myself and paid a price for not showing up for myself. However, I took every opportunity to learn something even if it was something I had already learned, I may have needed to learn it with a different understanding or I needed to recognize I didn't learn what was needed the first times.

Don't ever be hard on yourself for not showing up for yourself like you envision you would. Take your time and build up to it. Find you a Goal Friend set yourself some Journey Agreements and find inspiration within "you" to show up for yourself and be the best intentional you that current version of you needs.

One of the things I love about being intentional is that there is space to be intentional about doing nothing. We can get so consumed with this world trying to keep up and stay socially relevant that we forget who we are at our core and trust me I get it we can look up and see so many people showing up for themselves making things happen and 9 times out of 10 they are not sharing all that it took for them to show up as the person you see on the surface, and quite frankly they do not have too... Just do not be fooled by the glitz & glam surface level stories.

There is a point in this journey where we must strip ourselves down and simply "be". In this time, we must open ourselves to ourselves. It sounds confusing, but it's kind of like when a person tells a lie so long, they begin to believe it... We must create a safe space within our own realm and cultivate the true relationship with ourselves. Then share this person with the world... with boundaries!

Crying in this journey is normal and not crying in this journey is normal too. We are all wired differently, keep this in mind when assessing the family members and friends who can be there for you when you need a breaking moment or when you need a celebratory moment. Here is what I believe... We should have relationships where we can be free to express who we are with genuine feedback and openness. The way healthcare is - not everyone can afford a therapist. Therefore, also keep in mind our friends are not therapist, but genuine love, genuine friendship is therapy for the heart, soul, and mind, if you let it be.

Lastly, romantically, or platonically let people love you in the healthiest ways possible. No matter what, find peace and trust during your healing process or in general to love with an open heart and keep your heart open to the possibilities of being loved.

One of the things I love about me is that when I love people, I have no problem doing it wholeheartedly. Now, there are cons to this... We'll get into that in the next book, but for now I want you to know that I love you and I thank you for joining me in this intentional journey in showing up for ourselves...

I cannot wait to see what happens for you!

With love,

Shakeyla M. Ingram

95

THE PRAYER

God,

I know that You have only good things in store for me. And I know that you have brought me this far as a starting point for all if the greater experiences yet to come. And I know you didn't bring me this far, just to come this far.

Right here and right now, I come to you, knowing that all that I could ever dream up is because of you, every intention, every idea, every insight, every inspiration, and motivation.

BLESS MY VISION, BLESS MY DREAM

You know the hard work, determination, and commitment that I have invested. You know the excitement, the passion, and the dedication that I have. And you know I am willing and able to take the next steps to intentionally see this vision, this dream through.

I thank you God, because everything that I have accomplished and all that I am is because of you. I thank you for when I prayed for hard times to get easier, you made me stronger, and I thank you for always leading me on the right paths and filling me with the grace and strength to stay on the course.

All I can say is Thank You, Amen!

99

SIMPLE REMINDERS

Hey Goal Friend,

I wanted to leave you with some of my favorite simple reminders that I use to reflect on for whatever the occasion may call.... Some of the reminders are from me speaking to you, some are for you to say aloud to yourself and out into the universe, and some are for "us" so you know you are not alone.

You may have seen me share these on my social platforms... Just some extra kick to back you up when showing up for yourself... enjoy...

Simple Reminder #1

Even if, you may be overwhelmed
by all that is happening around you,
know your journey is going to be fulfilled
in the way that is best for "you".

Know you are not alone in this journey.

You will continue to grow beautifully
in your own timing and own way.

And everything will turn out
better than you ever expected.

I love you!

Simple Reminder #2

Some of us have been pulling
ourselves out of dark places alone;
probably since we were kids - there
were probably no role models,
but that doesn't matter if we're built different.

This is your reminder
that we CAN handle anything.

No matter what life has thrown at us…

It's all about all about how we
see ourselves showing up...

Simple Reminder #3

We must refuse to ever allow someone to take us back to a level that we have already leveled up from.

No one can ever make us fall for something we have risen from.

Nobody could ever make us deal with something that we have been done with.

Simple Reminder #4

It's not my job to show up for you as
some watered-down version of myself
that you deem acceptable.

My only duty is to show up as
my most authentic self and to
love and accept myself in each moment…

And with that you don't have to accept me,
but to those that do, Thank you!

Simple Reminder #5

Never let anyone gaslight you into believing that nurturing & standing up yourself is divisive.

You have the right to live your life...

Simple Reminder #6

The people who are purposed
to be in your life will never have to be
chased, begged, or given an ultimatum.

& that's on Love…

Simple Reminder #7

There's power in your presence!

Never forget that AND never allow
anyone to trick you into thinking otherwise.

And if they don't like your presence...

Then that's between them and God.

Simple Reminder #8

Learn to slow down and take care of yourself
before you're forced to do so.

Your emotional health matters,
your mental health matters,
your physical health matters,
and because all of those are connected
overall…

YOU MATTER.

Simple Reminder #9

You are more important than you believe.

Simple Reminder #10

In anything you do...

Make sure your heart is okay
and make sure your heart is in it.

Make sure your mind is okay
and your mind is in it, because
if the two are not in alignment...

You or it won't prosper...

Simple Reminder #11

I don't care how many people
appear to do what I do.

They don't do it like me.

They don't do it with my
brain, my ethics, my values, or my heart...

As you evolve you will make
a lot of people uncomfortable...

EVOLVE ANYWAY!

Simple Reminder #12

Respect your body when it
is asking for a break.

Respect your mind when it seeks rest.

Respect your soul when it
reminds you that you are whole.

Simple Reminder #13

No matter how good of person you are,
you are evil in someone's story.

Continue doing you,
speaking the truth and leveling up.

Simple Reminder #14

People telling you that you can't
do something are speaking
from their perspective.

They can't see you achieving
your goals and more importantly
they can't see it for themselves.

They judge based on their own
capability, perceived or actual.

Stay true to yourself and your vision.

Simple Reminder #15

Every once in a while,
someone amazing comes
into your life and boom…

 There you are!

Simple Reminder #16

Life is like the body, sometimes you need
to move in new ways for the pain to go away.

Move forward while remembering
that new habits equal a new life.

Simple Reminder #17

Other people are not your competition.

Your competition is the limiting
beliefs you are nurturing,
the dreams you are starving,
the fears you are feeding,
the lessons you reject,
the reflections you deflect,
and the signs you ignore.

Get out of your own way…

Simple Reminder #18

Never let anyone bring you down
with their perception of what they
think you should look like.

You will forever be lost in trying to find you.

Simple Reminder #19

A truly wise person knows that despite how much they know, there is ALWAYS so much more to learn and because of this, they view all situations as lessons.

Simple Reminder #20

Yeah, you should love and embrace
Who you currently are, however, remember
to hold space to continue discovering yourself
as well; retain new information, do not be
afraid of change and keep growing.

Simple Reminder #21

Be true to you, for you.

Simple Reminder #22

Keep your heart open.

Simple Reminder #23

Stop inviting unnecessary people into your space.

Period.

Simple Reminder #24

Own who you are,
don't fold, bend, break or shrink...

It's extremely imperative
for you to own every inch of you!

All you have to do is be you!

Somebody gone feel it!

And if they don't, then baby they don't!

Simple Reminder #25

You deserve a peaceful life.

Dismiss dem' people and keep it moving.

Simple Reminder #26

You NEVER have to prove to anyone that God doesn't play about his children.

Just sit back and be covered…

Simple Reminder #27

Sometimes we survive things and talk about it.

Sometimes we survive things and go silent.

Sometimes we survive things and create.

Each person deals with unimaginable pain their own way, and each person is entitled to that, without judgement...

Simple Reminder #28

It's okay for you to be the
highlight of your day!

Simple Reminder #29

Speak to yourself kindly while dealing with difficult situations.

Choose your battles wisely.

Peacefully step away from events, conversations, and interactions when your energy is being drained.

Take time to meditate.

Simple Reminder #30

Never have shame in who you are,
where you come from or your truth...

More importantly never allow
anyone to make you feel shameful.

You're not perfect and that should
never be your goal...

Your goal is to do and be better!

And you do this by
 learning, growing, knowing you better.

You will have lower days than most and you
will have higher days than most, but that all is a
part of the design of life.

Simple Reminder #31

Get back to the things that bring you Joy...

By any means necessary...

Simple Reminder #32

You are a garden.

Keep watering yourself so you can grow.

Simple Reminder #33

Baby steps do add up.

Simple Reminder #34

The right people will always
love you for exactly who you truly are.

Please do not pretend to be
something you are not.

Simple Reminder #35

Choose to show up authentically with
transparency and honesty regardless of
how others respond.

Simple Reminder #36

Stay solid.

Simple Reminder #37

Choose every day to forgive yourself.

You are human, flawed, and worthy of love.

Forgive yourself for not
knowing better at the time.

Forgive yourself for ignoring your intuition.

Forgive yourself for the survival patterns &
traits you picked up while experiencing abuse.

Simple Reminder #38

Take a moment to give thanks for the unseen.

Simple Reminder #39

Never forget that what a person
thinks of you is none of your business.

It's their thoughts...
let them keep em' and keep it moving.

Simple Reminder #40

When someone tries to trigger you,
turn off your ego.

If you are easily offended,
then it can lead to you being easily manipulated.

Simple Reminder #41

Happiness is a choice and not a result.

Nothing will make you happy unless you choose to be happy. Not one person will make you happy unless you decide to be happy within yourself.

Happiness doesn't come to you;
it comes from you.

Remember, you are the source to
your own happiness.

Simple Reminder #42

The secret weapon is an
open heart filled with love.

Simple Reminder #43

It's necessary to remember that
not everyone has it together, therefore,
there's no need to act like you do.

Acting like you do weighs
heavily on your mental health.

Surround yourself friends who can show you
how to live life, be happy, fail, succeed,
and still not have it all together.

Simple Reminder #44

Forward is forward.

Simple Reminder #45

Let yourself change and evolve.

You are allowed to outgrow the past.

Simple Reminder #46

When we are growing spiritually,
our ego will completely panic,
because our souls are pushing for change
to have better lives, better relationships,
better energies, better faith, and better health.

Continue to press forward.

Simple Reminder #47

Everything you go through is to ultimately bring you back home to yourself, everything.

Simple Reminder #48

Trust the process.

Understand the process.

Allow the process to unfold.

Being patient is a form of self-love.

Simple Reminder #49

You glow differently when
you only respond to love.

Simple Reminder #50

It's okay to enter a season of
prioritization & reflection instead of action.

Simple Reminder #51

If you're doing something to better yourself
and you disappoint someone else in the
process, know that it's okay.

You are not responsible for other
people's feelings about you, they are.

When you're in tune with yourself you'll always
know what's best for you and your healing.

So when I say "That's a you problem" or
"That's a them problem" ...

that's exactly what I mean.

Simple Reminder #52

Let's stop giving others the
power to decide who YOU are
and what YOUR reality looks like.

Only YOU can do that!

Simple Reminder #53

Everything you go through is to ultimately bring you back home to yourself.

Simple Reminder #54

Your mind is the battle ground.

It is the place where the greatest conflict is.

Save your mind over anything else...

Reach out to others...
ask for a non-judgmental safe space...

speak your truth

Simple Reminder #55

There is no right or wrong way to
feel about what you are experiencing.

Hold on to your faith system
and do what is necessary for YOU
to make it through this.

P.S.

I love you, I care about you,
and I'm thinking of you.

Simple Reminder #56

We must learn to see
lessons in each situation.

Sometimes things don't affect
us the same way as they used to.

We then begin to grow through
each thing we go through, we start
shifting our energy to create what we want,
and we stop worrying about
what we cannot control.

Simple Reminder #57

I'm going into a season where
intense grounding is needed.

This type of transition always makes
me nervous and scares me, but I aways
pull through with a grand finish.

Simple Reminder #58

We can sometimes doubt our growth when preparing to make a leap of faith.

Stand strong and flourish.

Simple Reminder #59

Being less reactive increases our growth and decreases stress.

Simple Reminder #60

Whatever you do in life...
let it be genuine... the rest will follow!

Simple Reminder #61

Let whoever think whatever...

Simple Reminder #62

Discipline over feelings leads to
achievements you can be proud of.

When you beat the mind, you can win the war.

Simple Reminder #63

The ability to catch yourself in
mid toxic behavior is major growth.

Simple Reminder #64

Our test of strength is
how we treat people
who mistreat us.

Simple Reminder #65

People love to hold grudges
against you for the things they did to you.

Don't be fooled. It's them, not you…

Simple Reminder #66

Only you can define you…

No one else!

Simple Reminder #67

Let's not learn the hard way to not allow people pull us into their storms.

At best, lets pull them into our peace.

If it's worth it…

Simple Reminder #68

Do not allow people to educate you based on what their motives are.

Simple Reminder #69

Creating from our soul, versus our ego, will look and feel different.

Simple Reminder #70

Kick back & observe, recognize that nothing out here is worth us getting out of character.

Simple Reminder #71

In order for us to heal,
a part of it must include understanding
why we felt what we did and why
we no longer need to feel it.

Understanding ourselves is key.

Know thyself = the essence of healing.

Simple Reminder #72

When you don't know where you're going, distractions look like opportunities.

Simple Reminder #73

Putting yourself first is not selfish,
it's mandatory & necessary.

With this you begin to give the world
the best of you, and not what's left of you.

Simple Reminder #74

Don't ask for Gods will to be done
then wonder why people start to disappear.

Your environment is shifting beloved.

Simple Reminder #75

Receiving with abundance doesn't
happen when you're full of yourself.

Our ego is only our enemy
when it's out of control.

Allow your soul to lead and watch
how you become driven by a healthy
self-love & ego, that will make room
for you to receive abundance.

Simple Reminder #76

It's better to work on ourselves
because we love ourselves,
not because we hate who we are,
or because we think we will be
rewarded a relationship.

Love, hate, and despair come
with their own vibration.

Simple Reminder #77

Sometimes you've gotta work the system just as hard as it's working you.

Simple Reminder #78

You are the only person that will feel your pain.

So, help yourself by letting it out, allow your heart to be clear, and move forward choosing peace & love over everything.

Know, it's perfectly okay to just be done.

Not mad, not upset or angry.

Done.

We must remember our lives are of value.

Simple Reminder #79

Let us learn how to direct and focus
our mental and emotional energy.

Don't become blind or fully out of touch
with the world, but also don't become so
distracted with all that is going on within it
that we lose sight of the individual purpose
we were chosen for.

Simple Reminder #80

You attract what you think and feel.

Don't allow the negative thoughts to block positivity from entering your life.

Simple Reminder #81

Self-love is not just cutting toxic people from your life, but also cutting ties with the version of yourself who allowed that toxic energy to continue for as long as it did.

Playing the victim will only blind you to your own flaws and create unilateral misery and toxic cycles.

Simple Reminder #82

Ignoring drama, pettiness, and negative comments is not a show of weakness...

It's spiritual leadership

Simple Reminder #83

Sometimes we have to let people who
protect and feed off their insecurities
believe they have won because the truth is…

They can never win until they've
made peace with what's within.

Simple Reminder #84

Remember to be mindful of what you
take in emotionally, spiritually, and physically.

Simple Reminder #85

Our wounds cannot heal under masks…

They need air…

Simple Reminder #86

What we don't repair, we repeat.

Simple Reminder #87

To be true to the person you are becoming requires you to be proud of who you are.

Never discredit what you endured on your path of self-discovery.

Simple Reminder #88

If you don't commit to anything one person will come and tell you to do this, another person will come and tell you to do that and you won't have time for yourself.

Commitment is the key to freedom.

Simple Reminder #89

Trauma: change you do not choose
Healing: change that you do choose

Simple Reminder #90

We often overestimate things we are capable of in addition to underestimating others. The human mind can be great at calculations but is not so great at predicting our own potential.

However, when we need to find strength, it's most likely that we will find it outside of ourselves. This may be in spirituality or religion, in relationships, or simply in the words of others who have come before us and faced similar struggles.

Tough times are inevitable, but if we recognize that we can do so, and we are prepared… we can grow as people and go on to push the boundaries and experience a richer and more fulfilling life.

Ps. I'm rooting for you!

Simple Reminder #91

Be open and honest with yourself about what it is you want in this life.

Do not deny any chance at your dreams.

Allow your faith to be large than your fears.

Simple Reminder #92

It's too easy to get caught up in a sea of emotions and brought down to a feeling of bitterness.

However, when you continuously work on yourself, love on yourself, and remember to be gentle with yourself - it becomes easier to not even allow those emotions overwhelm you and get embed within you.

Don't let your hard work go to waste!

Simple Reminder #93

You were not meant to hustle
every second of every day.

A rested mind and body can
accomplish more than a weary one.

Simple Reminder #94

I'm getting better at transforming
my burdens into blessings.

Simple Reminder #95

Kindness is not always associated with strength, but it is always the strongest people who are able to be the kindest - they typically don't feel a need to be on the defense or throw up barriers to provide protection for themselves.

They offer genuine kindness because they are safe with who they are.

As a caveat, something people should understand about the extremely kind, nice, & loving people, is that the other side of them is just as extreme.

It is the hell they have survived that makes them so gentle & loving. Therefore, never mistake their self-control for weakness.

The beast within them is sleeping, not dead...

Simple Reminder #96

I am consistently striving to evolve into the best version of myself spiritually & mentally, not by competing with others, but by reflecting on my own evolution.

I seek solitude as my refuge, my safe haven...

It is where I recharge + recollect.

Simple Reminder #97

No one is holier than thou.

No one is "more spiritual" than the other.

Spirituality and self-discovery is not a race.

The path of your true self is a path of connection, unconditional love, acceptance of the now, rawness, vulnerability, and humility.

It is not an ego battle.

Simple Reminder #98

What we are doing is overcoming...
Preparing ourselves for what's to come...

Loving ourselves in new ways...

And healing myself in new ways...

Simple Reminder #99

Life is too precious to have people around us
that don't value our existence.

They gotta go…

Simple Reminder #100

You don't want to be gone from this world.

You simply want your life as you
currently know it to end.

The path your life is on can always change in an
instant.

It's the deliberate act of letting go of what
no longer serves you that really changes
everything for your reality.

You must create space for the
frequency of the reality you truly want.

We can do it!

INTENTIONALLY HERE

Q: Is showing up for yourself worth it?

A: Yes

ABOUT THE AUTHOR

Shakeyla M. Ingram is a vocal leader and entrepreneur who believes in standing up for what's right and advocating for others. She currently serves as an elected official in her hometown of Fayetteville, NC.

Friends, family, colleagues, and associates recognize Shakeyla for her positive energy and consistency in showing up as a loving driven, and supportive individual.

Shakeyla is also a Marketing, Wellness and Community Relations enthusiast. As the founder and president of her consulting firm she focuses on empowering small businesses to know and believe their business can have an impact and scale through a strong and innovative marking plan. Shakeyla is most known for her advisory roles and event production work with local organizations. She not only focuses on marketing, but she also ensures that each business owner she works with understands their room for expansion and how to act on it with mindfulness, balance, and confidence.

Shakeyla currently resides in North Carolina and can be contacted by email for speaking/booking requests:

E-mail: shakeylaingram@gmail.com
Facebook: Shakeyla M. Ingram
Instagram: @shakeylaingram

Intentionally Here

Here's what happens when you show up for yourself.

SHAKEYLA M. INGRAM